encyclopedia

# ENCYCLOPEDIA

rachel
jendrzejewski

Spout Press
Minneapolis, MN

encyclopedia
Rachel Jendrzejewski

ISBN 978-0-9835478-3-9


First Edition
Printed in the United States of America


All encyclopedia entries are adapted from
*Encyclopedia Americana*, 2001 edition,
and used by permission


Spout Press is a member of CLMP and is distributed to the trade
by Small Press Distribution, Berkeley, CA
(www.spdbooks.org)




Published by
Spout Press
P.O. Box 581067
Minneapolis, MN 55458-1067

"Reality is a sound, you have to tune in to it
not just keep yelling."

—Anne Carson, *Autobiography of Red*

# DEVELOPMENT HISTORY

*encyclopedia* received a workshop production in February 2010 in Providence, RI, at Rhode Island School of Design's Fleet Library as part of the Brown University Writing is Live Festival (Head of Writing for Performance: Erik Ehn; Festival Producer: Vanessa Gilbert). It was directed by Shana Gozansky. Cast: Lauren Lubow (Lua), Lauren Neal (Dal). Sound: Peter Wood. Stage Manager: Kate Rourke.

*encyclopedia* received a staged reading in January 2012 in Los Angeles, CA, at Lot 613, presented by Padua Playwrights (Artistic Director: Guy Zimmerman) and made possible by an Emergency Grant from The Foundation for Contemporary Arts, as part of the Downtown Arts District Winterfest. It was directed by Shishir Kurup. Cast: Nicole Gabriella Scipione (Lua), Lina Patel (Dal). Music: Brad Culver, Andrew Gilbert. Lighting Design: Dan Reed. Stage Manager: Amanda Mauer.

*encyclopedia* received a staged reading in January 2016 in Minneapolis, MN, at The Playwrights' Center as part of the Ruth Easton New Play Series (Producing Artistic Director: Jeremy Cohen; Associate Artistic Director: Hayley Finn). It was directed by Emily Mendelsohn. Cast: Sun Mee Chomet (Lua), Megan Burns (Dal). Music: Crystal Myslajek, Chris Hepola. Intern/Stage Manager: Ana Puente Cackley.

characters:
DAL
LUA

Both roles are female.
Both names mean "moon."
Both characters are grounded in their
respective realities.

setting:
A neglected kitchen
A neglected field

time:
now

notes:
The symbol "//" signals the next line is
interrupting.

Music should function as a third voice in this text.
As Lua and Dal attempt to use words, the music
insists that words don't suffice. Sound "cues" in the
script (rain, clock, static, etc.) should be treated as
prompts for music, rather than literal sound effects.
Substantial swells of sound should unfold between
most scenes.

# ENCYCLOPEDIA

## SCENE 1

*DAL stands in a field, holding an enormous umbrella. She is hardly visible, as rain pours down all sides of the umbrella.*

*LUA addresses the audience.*

LUA
This is a farmhouse.
That is a field.
This is a window, overlooking the field.
That is rain.

This is a prelude to the new moon.

Throughout the night,
you may hear a click.
The click of a clock.
Time is passing.
Is the time on that clock right?

What time is right?

What I really want to tell you is—*(she smiles)*

This is a prelude to the new moon.

Throughout the night,
you may hear the clock continuously.
The click of the clock may replace words.
Words may replace the click.
The click might be imaginary.
The click might interfere.
You or I might interfere with the click.

*She laughs a little too loudly.*

LUA
What am I talking about?
What can I say?
Time is passing.

What I really want to tell you is—*(she smiles)*

This is a neglected farmhouse.
That is a neglected field.
This is a neglected kitchen.

This is a prelude to the new moon.
This is how the prelude goes.
It is instrumental.

This is how it goes:
Phase
Phase
A phase
Phase
A phase

*The click of a clock.*

LUA
Throughout the night,
you may hear the click constantly.
You may never hear the click.
The click might be imaginary.
What can I say?

Phase
Phase
A phase
Phase
A phase

What I really want to tell you is—

This is a prelude to the new moon.

This is a prelude.

A click.

This is a phase.
A click that may replace words.

This is a farmhouse.
A prelude.

A neglected kitchen.
A click.
What can I say?
Time is passing.
A phase.
Phase
A phase
Phase
A phase
Phase
Phase
A phase

Phase
A phase
Phase
Phase
A phase
Phase
A phase
Phase
Phase
A phase
Phase
A phase
Phase
Phase
A phase
*(etc.)*

*The rain becomes stronger.*

*LUA's words loop for a long time.*
*They blend with the rain.*

*Eventually, the rain and words die down,*
*then stop completely.*

*DAL becomes visible under her umbrella.*

9

## SCENE 2

*New Moon.*

DAL
I organize my senses into balloons.

*She pulls five helium balloons out from under her umbrella.*

DAL
I put my senses inside.
They are valentines.
My sense of sight goes first, in pink.

*She releases a balloon to the sky.*
*It floats, disappears.*

DAL
My sense of smell goes second, in orange.

*She releases a balloon.*
*It floats, disappears.*

DAL
My sense of taste goes third, in green.

*She releases a balloon.*
*It floats, disappears.*

DAL
My sense of hearing goes fourth, in yellow.

*She releases a balloon.*
*It floats, disappears.*

DAL
My sense of touch goes last, in blue.

*She releases a balloon.*
*It floats, disappears.*

DAL
I think about everything.
I'm emptied of everything.

*Undercurrents, enveloping*

SCENE 3

*DAL moves inside and opens an encyclopedia.*
*LUA moves outside and puts away the umbrella.*
*At different moments, they each glance up,*
*looking for the moon.*

DAL
Encyclopedia Americana.
Oporto to Photoengraving, page 854.
Phase.
An entry composed by Fergus J. Wood
of the National Oceanographic Survey.
Phase.
In astronomy, the changing luminous configuration
of the moon,
or of a planet in an orbit near both earth and sun,
produced by varying amounts of sunlight reflected
from it toward the earth.
When the moon is directly between the earth
and the sun,
only its far side is illuminated and—

*LUA breezes into the kitchen.*

LUA
(nonchalant)
The moon is invisible.

*She begins banging around in cupboards, looking for dishes.*

DAL
This is called the new moon.
As the moon continues in its orbital motion around
the earth,
a crescent-shaped portion of its western edge is
illuminated by the sun's rays.
This is the crescent after new phase.
At a position one-quarter of the way around
the earth
(first-quarter phase),
one-half of the moon's apparent disk appears
bright.
Further orbital motion produces the gibbous phase,
as more than one-half but not all of the moon's
disk is illuminated.

LUA
Are you hungry?

DAL
As the moon reaches a position directly opposite
the earth from the sun
(but not in the plane of the ecliptic—a lunar
eclipse),
its entire disk shines and is known as full moon.
Thereafter, as the eastern portion of the moon
becomes sunlit instead of the western,
the cycle of phases is repeated in reverse order
from gibbous to last-quarter to
crescent-before-new
and back to new moon again.

*She skims down the page.*

DAL
The average time between two new moons
is 29 days, 12 hours, and 44 minutes.

LUA
Why would you bother with an outdated book
when you've got everything current online?

DAL
The average time between two new moons
is 29 days, 12 hours, and 44 minutes.

*LUA bangs and clangs pots and pans.*
*She pulls out a soup pot, a knife, and cutting board.*

## SCENE 4

*Waxing Crescent Moon.*
*LUA makes soup from scratch.*
*She chops vegetables with remarkable speed and precision.*
*She addresses the audience.*

| LUA | DAL |
|---|---|
| That is Dal. | |
| The word "dal" is Korean. | |
| It means "moon." | |
| I am told that | |
| 29 days, 12 hours, | 29 days, 12 hours, |
| and 44 minutes ago, | and 44 minutes ago, |
| a gun went off. | |
| *(loud gossipy faux whisper)* | a planet exploded. |
| The love of her life was killed. | |
| | On television. |
| Overseas, in the war. | |
| One of the wars. | |
| So tragic! | Your ashes are |
| | scattered |
| | in outer space. |

Honestly, I don't
totally understand
the whole story,
what happened
exactly
but it's clear that

Dal has not been able
to accept the situation.
Her state of being
can no longer be
categorized as grief.
I believe she has spiraled

into

some kind of
mental disorder.

Often, she can't even
brush her teeth
by herself.
I am here to
take care of her.

I don't understand—
I don't know—

I don't know—

You weren't able—

I don't accept
this state—

How to—

Your body is orbiting
the earth right now,
in fragments.

A mental picture
fading—
I already can't quite

remember your teeth.

I had promised
to take care of you.

Sometimes, it seems
she can understand
language, but not
its tone, its feeling.
Its subtext.

More often, it seems
she's telling herself
private stories.

She can understand
tone and feeling

but not meaning.

There are, shall we say,
intense moments.

Ups and downs.

Some days are
better than others.

Sometimes, it seems

(from afar,
like a feeling)
you can understand
language.

More often, it seems

they're making
up stories about you.

Primary colors.
You would laugh.

Your face in a million
tiny colored dots—

Like a light—
Like a map—

Like drifting—

We are exploring the
many possibilities
of what might be wrong.

Dal has problems
articulating what
she wants to say.
Problems with
language comprehension.
Her thinking is scattered.
Loss of memory.
Loss of discernment.
Derealization.
She fabricates stories
that don't make sense.

She embellishes the truth.
She is a muddle
of symptoms.
We are experimenting
with different medications.
When she opens
her mouth,
jumbles of letters fall out.

Like music—
Like monuments—
Like possibilities—
Like planets, plants—
Like marbles—

Like staring—
Like promise—
Like tunnels—
Like fast in a car—
Like memory—
Like yellow green pink—
Like gold—
Like fabric, swatches—
No, that doesn't
make sense.
Your truth—

I think—
I know I—
I just think I—

*DAL opens her mouth.*
*Thousands of blocky clunky letters pour out.*

LUA
She does not know how to articulate coherent thoughts.
When she opens her mouth,
chaos pours out.

*DAL opens her mouth.*
*A marching band pours out.*
*A frenzied parade takes over the farm—*
*Dancers. Fire-eaters. Stilts. Puppets. Juggling. Unicycles.*
*The world is engulfed for maybe 10 seconds.*
*Then all the activity disperses as quickly as it appeared.*

*It is raining again.*
*DAL is drenched.*

*LUA's soup preparation has fast-forwarded to a finish.*
*A pot of soup simmers on the stove.*
*LUA serves it into a bowl.*

DAL
For the past month,
it's been raining saltwater.

# SCENE 5

*DAL stares at LUA, bewildered.*

DAL
Who are you?

LUA
You know who I am.

DAL
I live here.
This is my house.
I don't know who you are.
You're trespassing in my house.

LUA
This is my house, too.
I live here with you.

DAL
This is my house.

LUA
Your hands are all muddy.
There's mud on your face.

Here, let me set this down.
I have a towel.

DAL
I don't need a towel.
You're trespassing in my house.
I don't know who you are.

LUA
Honey, you do.
You know who I am.

*She glances at the audience and laughs a little too loudly.*

LUA
(*to DAL*)
I am here, day and night.
I clean and narrate.
I clean up and narrate your life.
It's very important that I do this.
I'm extracting the jumble from your brain.
I'm creating space for cognition.

DAL
I have plenty of space.

LUA
I'm here to compartmentalize.
To categorize.
To help you think.
I'm here to sweep.
I'm here to vacuum.
Come on.
You know this.

*Distant birds, wings.*

DAL
I don't need anything vacuumed.

LUA
I made some soup.

DAL
I think—

LUA
Are you hungry?

DAL
No. I think—
I think that—

LUA
What?

DAL
I don't—
I mean I think—

LUA
Yes?

DAL
I just—

LUA
What are you trying to say?

DAL
I—

LUA
What? Yes? What is it?
Look, I think you
should just—

DAL
I think that—
What I really
want to tell you is—

DAL
That encyclopedia and I are looking at each other
with—
We know we can never fully absorb // one another—

LUA
You're shivering.
You're wet.
Would you like a bigger towel?
Let me get you a bigger towel.

# SCENE 6

*First Quarter Moon.*
*The rain is dissipating.*
*LUA looks for a towel.*
*DAL opens an encyclopedia.*

DAL
Encyclopedia Americana.
Trance to Venial Sin, page 854.
Vacuum.
An entry composed by M. H. Hablanian of the
Varian/Lexington Vacuum Division.
Vacuum.
Space without matter.
The concept of vacuum has two different
meanings.
One refers to complete emptiness—
specifically, to space without air.
An example is intergalactic space.
The other refers to air or other gases in which
the pressure is lower than the atmospheric
pressure.
An example is the reduced pressure
at the inlet of a vacuum cleaner
or in a drinking straw.

*She skims down the page.*

DAL
Vacuums in Everyday Life.
The most common example of partial vacuum
involves human breathing.
Expanding the lungs increases their volume.
This creates a pressure slightly lower than that in
the atmosphere
and permits additional air to enter the lungs.

*She skims further.*

DAL
Characteristics of a Vacuum Environment.
Under a high degree of vacuum,
an animal cannot survive more than a few seconds
of exposure,
fire will not burn,
sound will not exist,
volatile liquids will evaporate at a high rate,
and lubricating surfaces such as graphite may
become abrasive
owing to the loss of absorbed water.
However, the transmission

of light and radio waves is unaffected
or even improved by the absence of matter.

*LUA returns with a large bath towel.*

LUA
Please come out from under the table.

*DAL shuts the book.*

LUA
Please come out from under the table.
You should come out and eat something.
Come on.

*LUA makes a great, valiant effort.*

LUA
There we go!

*DAL stares at the soup.*
*LUA goes to the sink and washes the pot.*

LUA
(*to the audience*)
Dal does not know how to communicate.
She does not know how to listen.

This misfortune is not her fault;
something simply went wrong in her brain.
Listening, of course, is a privilege,
an acquired skill that can only be maintained
by those of us whose neurons and families
are in certain categories from the start.
My name is Lua.
The word "lua" is Portuguese. It means "moon."
I am lucky to be a very privileged person.
I am lucky to be a very, very good listener.

DAL
Today I realized we wouldn't go grocery shopping
together anymore.
When people stop grocery shopping together,
an ocean forms between them.

LUA
Dal is somewhat but not quite fully aware that
her brain is crowded.
Crowded, crowded, crowded with words.

DAL
It's like I was on a boat facing you,
but pulled in the other direction.

LUA

The words in her mind dissolve and merge
with the words that she hears and reads,
the way fluids blend and bleed into each other.
This creates a mental flood:
a natural disaster
which continuously spills out of her mouth.

DAL

I could see you, talking.
I could see words, letters, tumbling out of your
mouth,
but I couldn't understand what you were saying.

LUA

When she sleeps, she dreams in streaming text.
And when she's awake, I'm afraid to say,
she is simply a sea of nonsense.

DAL

I could see shapes in your face.
I drifted in my boat and watched everything
around you explode.
Green. Indigo. Yellow. Gold. Pink. Red. Turquoise.
Black. Peach. Orange. Blue. Brown.

LUA
The problem is, evolution stopped a long time ago.

DAL
And now—

LUA
I mean, where do we go from here?

DAL
Looking through shadows—
What food makes sense—

LUA
I mean, look at her.

DAL
Can you hear anything?

LUA
Quite frankly, I am at a loss.

DAL
Can you see anything?

LUA
Quite frankly, she is deteriorating.

DAL
I'll make a space—

LUA
Quite frankly, this property ought to be sold.
She is too dysfunctional to maintain it alone.

# SCENE 7

*LUA clears the table.*
*She finds a broom and sweeps the kitchen floor,*
*vigorously, methodically, like clockwork.*
*She never stops the motion of sweeping, even when she speaks.*

LUA
(*to the audience*)
Once in awhile, we have lucid conversations.
You should be aware, however, that everything she
says is delusional.

DAL
I went for a walk in the cemetery this morning.

LUA
Oh, did you?

DAL
I walked around for an hour.
Wasted so much time.
Smoked cigarettes, one after another.

LUA
You don't smoke.

*LUA gives the audience a knowing smile.*

DAL
A couple asked me if I needed directions.
If I was looking for a specific plot.
I said no, but they kept prodding, insisting.
I hate helpful strangers.

LUA
Were you looking for a specific plot?

DAL
They have an automated computer system there.
Like an ATM, only it's an index of dead people.
You can punch in the last name of the person
whose grave you want to visit,
and the machine will show you a map of how to
get to the exact spot.
You can print the map for free.

LUA
*(to the audience)*
Nothing's free, dear, sorry to say.

*LUA laughs a little too loudly.*

DAL
The whole computer system thing is strange,
but also kind of nice.
Like a phonebook.
As if you could just call each person up.
Plus, that place is endless.
I had no idea.
It would be hard to find anyone specific without
that system.

*LUA sweeps faster.*

DAL
Anyway, I picked a name at random.
It turned out to be a woman who died in 1899.
I printed the map, and I went to find her.

LUA
I don't know how it gets so dirty in here.

DAL
The weird thing is, when I got there,
there were fresh flowers on her grave.
She died in 1899, but there were fresh flowers on
her grave,

like someone just left them there today,
like someone had visited her just before I did.

LUA
I swear I just did this floor—

DAL
Who would still be leaving flowers for someone
who died in 1899?

LUA
And look how awful—

DAL
It made me want to bring someone flowers.
It made me // want to—

LUA
Watch your feet, hon.

*LUA sweeps faster.*

# SCENE 8

*Waxing Gibbous Moon.*
*LUA fills a bucket with water and starts*
*scrubbing the floor.*
*She never stops the motion of scrubbing,*
*even when she speaks.*

DAL
I chart a map of my sleep.
I draw continents of dreams.
Each one is an epitaph.

LUA
Oooh, are you starting a journal?
Like I suggested?
That is very good!
You understood something I said!
This is a very good step forward.
Very very very good.

DAL
Here, an asteroid.

LUA
Um… okay.
*(to the audience)*
I recently recommended that
Dal start keeping a journal.
I'm a firm believer that journaling is
an excellent way to Connect with one's Brain.

DAL
There, an image on repeat.
There, an animal in fast-forward.
There, a book.

LUA
I tried keeping a journal myself for some time,
but I could never really maintain the habit.
It's not really my thing.
But it certainly can do wonders for other people.
Especially people who have, you know, a certain
kind of Work to Do.

DAL
There, a commercial.
There, a water tower.
Here, a piano.
Here, an answering machine message.

There, the clunk of your words hitting the floor.

*LUA knocks something over.*
*She glances at the audience and laughs.*

LUA
Oops! Yikes!

*She cleans up, then resumes scrubbing, harder than before.*

LUA
Honestly, I just thought she should have
something to do.
It can be very difficult to motivate a person
in this condition
to do anything, really.

DAL
Here, a flock of birds.
There, a jacket.
There, a shopping cart.
Here, a glass boat.

LUA
And I'm just talking entertainment, passing the time.
Never mind functions that require responsibility.

I mean, especially if they live alone.
I mean, when you have someone this far gone—

DAL
Right here, a boat made of glass.

LUA
Who pays their bills?
What do you do with their mail?

DAL
I read that glass is // a form of matter—

LUA
It's a very delicate matter—

DAL
With solid, liquid, and gas state properties—

LUA
We do the best we can to help, but
it can all be very // exhausting, really,

DAL
What if it can—

LUA
very frustrating sometimes.
It can be difficult to maintain patience // really,
it—

DAL
I wonder if I could—

LUA
Can just be very frustrating, really,
very exhausting sometimes,
very // frustrating, because—

DAL
Solid, liquid, and gas—

LUA
At the end of the day—

DAL
Glass—

LUA
What really matters is—

*LUA accidentally knocks over the bucket of water.*

| LUA | DAL |
|---|---|
| Oh shit fuck damn—! | Oh—! |

*Water spills across the floor.*
*LUA tries to clean it up,*
*but more and more water keeps pouring out of the bucket.*
*She searches for towels, a mop, anything.*

*DAL stares at the widening pool.*
*She reaches deep down into it with both hands*
*and carefully pulls out a glass boat.*
*It is large enough for one person to sit inside.*
*She climbs in.*

*Water pours harder and faster out of the bucket.*
*It fills the whole kitchen.*
*It surrounds and lifts DAL's boat.*
*It becomes the ocean at spring tide.*

# SCENE 9

*The ocean takes over the entire space.*
*The waves are massive and rolling.*
*The sound is wholly engulfing.*
*A period of wild submersion,*
*followed by a subsiding to calm.*

# SCENE 10

*Full Moon.*
*DAL drifts through the ocean in her glass boat.*
*LUA follows on a boat made of broomsticks.*
*She leans across and puts a party hat on DAL's head.*

DAL
29 days, 12 hours, and 44 minutes ago,
I found myself at a birthday party.

LUA
A birthday party for Dal!
It is a lucid birthday party.

DAL
It is an uncertain birthday party.

LUA
*(loud, gossipy faux whisper to the audience)*
I am the only guest at the party.

DAL
This morning, I bought groceries for my birthday
party alone.

LUA
(*to DAL*)
I bought you a present. Here.

*She gives DAL a large umbrella.*

LUA
It's a flower.
You have to be careful with it though.
Don't crush it.

DAL
Thank you.

LUA
I bought you a present. Here.

*She gives DAL a huge stack of bedsheets.*

LUA
It's a clock.
You have to assemble it, though.
Don't hurt yourself.
I'll help you.

DAL
Thank you.

LUA
I bought you a present. Here.

*She gives DAL a gigantic, heavy box.*
*DAL opens it and pulls out an encyclopedia.*
*She pulls out encyclopedia after encyclopedia,*
*a brand new full set.*

LUA
It's a frame of reference.
You have to take care of it, though.
Don't neglect it.

*DAL carefully sets each book to float on the water.*

*LUA reaches into the ocean and pulls out a birthday cake.*
*It has a single unlit candle in the center.*

DAL
Full moon.
Big low full moon.
The big low full moon comes down to light the
candle on my cake.

*The candle lights.*

DAL
I blow the candle out and wish for—well of course,
I can't tell you.
I make the wish at 12:34 PM, 1-2-3-4.

*A clock ticks.*
*LUA blows out the candle.*

DAL
We toast to the future, empty glasses.
I try to make eye contact for good luck, but—

LUA
Yoo-hoo, where did you go?

DAL
A million tiny colored dots.

LUA
I bought you a present. Here.

*LUA produces a bundle of five helium balloons,*
*but does not give them to DAL.*

LUA
Five senses.
You have to take care of them though.
Are you going to lose them?

DAL
Are you going to lose them?

LUA
Are you going to lose them?

DAL
Are you going to lose them?

LUA
I'll keep them for you.

DAL
No—

LUA
I'll keep them for you.

DAL
No—

LUA
Happy birthday!

*The faint clamor of marching band in the distance, growing closer.*

DAL
What I really want to tell // you is—

LUA
Don't crush it.

DAL
What I really want to tell // you is—

LUA
Don't hurt yourself.

DAL
What I really want to tell // you is—

LUA
Don't neglect it.

DAL
What I really want to tell // you is—

LUA
Don't lose them.

DAL
What I really want // to tell you is—

LUA
Don't neglect it.

DAL
What I really want // to tell you is—

LUA
Don't hurt yourself.

DAL
What I really want // to tell you is—

LUA
Don't crush it.

DAL
What I really want // to tell you is—

LUA
Don't.

DAL & LUA
What I really want to tell you is—

LUA
Don't.

DAL & LUA
What I really want to tell you is—

*They are drowned out by the marching band and its*
*accompanying festivities,*
*all of which float by on a chaotically-crammed raft.*

# SCENE 11

*The water subsides.*
*The farm reappears, but things look different now.*
*The kitchen and field are less distinct from each other,*
*overlapping and merged.*
*The furniture is rearranged.*
*Encyclopedias are scattered everywhere.*
*The birthday bedsheets are folded on a table.*

*DAL watches the moon.*
*LUA is exhausted and tense,*
*but nevertheless gets to work cleaning up.*
*She stacks the encyclopedias as though trying to recreate*
*clear walls.*

LUA
*(Speaking briskly as she works)*
Lately, Dal has been having very alarming
hallucinations.
Her behavior is becoming more erratic.
It's impossible to categorize.
She is becoming less and less cooperative.
She is disturbed.
She is withdrawing.
She is irritable and aggressive.

She is not connecting things together.
She is imagining things that are not there.
She is not sleeping well.
She is not eating well.
She is not responding to medication.

*DAL opens an encyclopedia and reads.*

DAL
Encyclopedia Americana.
Russia to Skimmer, page 559.
Senses and Sensation.
An entry composed by Philburn Ratoosh of
the University of California at Berkeley.
Senses and Sensation.
Men have been concerned with the senses
as long as they have asked questions about
the nature of the world
and been self-conscious about the limitations
of their knowledge.

LUA
The problem is, evolution stopped a long time ago.

DAL
Classification of the Senses.

The senses can be classified in many ways.
They may, for example, be classified
by the kind of physical energy to which the end
organs are sensitive,
or by anatomical characteristics of the receptors
themselves,
or by the type of nerve that carries the impulses
from the receptor.
Thus, the question, "How many senses are there?"
has no single answer.
The number depends on how one wishes to
classify them.

*She frowns.*
*She skips ahead.*

LUA
I mean, where do we go from here?

DAL
Sensory Nerves.

LUA
I mean, look at her.

DAL
Since the sense organs differ so widely,
Responding as they do to different kinds
of physical energy,
the best place to find phenomena
common to all the senses
is in the sensory nerves—
the neural pathways that lead from the sensory
cells.

LUA
Quite frankly, she is deteriorating.

DAL
The threshold of any sensory system is
the least energy to which the system responds.

LUA
Quite frankly, I am at a loss.

DAL
When physical energy above the system's threshold
impinges on a sense organ,
the sense cells transform this energy into
electrical impulses,

action potentials,
in the sensory nerves.

*DAL closes the book in frustration.*

LUA
Quite frankly, she needs more specialized
supervision.
Quite frankly, this property ought to be sold.
She is too dysfunctional to maintain it alone.

*LUA takes the encyclopedia from DAL
and places it with the others.*

*The "wall" of encyclopedias is small and ineffective.*

## SCENE 12

*Waning Gibbous Moon.*

*Undercurrents, enveloping.*

*DAL falls asleep.*

*LUA goes to the window and shakily lights a cigarette.*
*She stares at the moon, smoking, fidgeting.*
*She smokes the entire cigarette.*
*She puts it out.*

*She sits on the floor, leaning against the kitchen counter.*
*She closes her eyes.*
*She falls asleep, too.*

*A long period of sleeping lull.*

*After some time, slowly and subtly,*
*the sound begins to cut in and out,*
*creating Morse code-like patterns.*

# SCENE 13

*A loud explosion.*
*DAL and LUA each wake with a start.*

DAL & LUA
I just had the most realistic dream.

DAL
You were there—

LUA
No, you had called—

DAL
You had called—

LUA
No, you had written—

DAL
The moon had written me a letter—

LUA
You had written me a letter from the moon.

*LUA takes a deep breath and lets it out.*
*DAL looks up at the sky.*

LUA
I'll help you with this.
Let me help you with this.

*LUA shakes out the bedsheets*
*and goes to work draping them over all the furniture.*
*She smoothes them, fixing each wrinkle and corner.*
*Her speech becomes increasingly measured and fierce.*

DAL
We chart a map of our sleep.
We draw continents of dreams.
Each one is a million epitaphs.

LUA
*(to the audience)*
This really is a difficult—

DAL
There, a string.
Here, a stone.
There, a light left on.

LUA
It's a tricky one.
It really is a tough // situation—

DAL
Here, a sensation of the alphabet.

LUA
A terribly tragic situation,
somebody losing somebody like that.
Someone having to go through, deal—
Someone // falling into—

DAL
There, a paradox.
Here, a parachute.

LUA
And it can all be very frustrating, really,
Very difficult to maintain patience // sometimes,
because—

DAL
Here, a valentine.
Here, a vitamin.

LUA
Well, it's very difficult to motivate a person in //
this condition—

DAL
Here, conditional—

LUA
The chemicals—

DAL
Here, an orbit.

LUA
She's limited in what we can—
Or she doesn't want—
She's just chemically—

DAL
Here, compounding.

LUA
We should be thankful for our good health.
We should be thankful for // our circumstances—

DAL
Here, a covering.

LUA
Most of us know how to cope with difficult
situations.

DAL
A covering of the moon.
Earth shadow.
Lunar eclipse.

LUA
Most of us do cope in a much more
balanced manner.
You allow yourself a short time and then
you pick up the pieces and move on.
Keep busy, keep busy, keep busy.
It's not actually that hard!
Not at the end of the day.
For most of us, anyway, for most of us.
There are so many good ways to keep busy.
You want my honest opinion,
I think she was too idle for too long,
I think that was // part of the—

DAL
Earth shadow.
Moon covering.

LUA
But of course, really, at the end of the day,
We all know this misfortune is not her fault;
something simply went wrong in her brain.

*LUA grasps for another chore to do.*
*DAL's gaze is fixed steadily on the moon.*

# SCENE 14

*Last Quarter Moon.*

*LUA sweeps the kitchen floor,*
*vigorously, methodically, like clockwork.*
*She never stops the motion of sweeping, even when she speaks.*

DAL
I went to the grocery store this morning.

LUA
That is simply not true.

DAL
I walked around for an hour.
Wasted so much time.
Just stacking things in a cart.
One thing after another.
Someone asked me if I needed assistance.
If I was looking for a specific aisle.
I said no but they kept following me around.
I hate helpful strangers.
Okay, I don't actually hate them.
I just wanted to be alone, you know?

LUA
I don't know how it gets so dirty in here.

DAL
They have an automated product search there.
A whole enormous index of food.
You can punch in the item you're looking for,
and the machine will tell you what aisle it's in.
Even the shelf that it's on.
You can print a map for free.

LUA
No such thing as free.

DAL
A map of how to get to that aisle and shelf
from where you are in the store!

LUA
This broom is horrible.

DAL
I picked an item at random, a certain soup.
The weird thing is, when I got to the aisle,
they were giving away samples of the soup
I'd picked.

There were probably more than a hundred different
soups, brands—
but they were giving away samples of the exact soup
I'd picked,
like someone had read my mind,
like someone had seen me randomly select it,
then ran and heated up a batch in the back.


LUA
I swear I just did this floor, and look, how awful—


DAL
It made me want to make somebody soup.


LUA
Watch your feet, hon.


*DAL takes a long look at the sheet-covered kitchen.*
*A clock ticks.*

# SCENE 15

*DAL reads an encyclopedia.*
*LUA puts out leftovers.*

DAL
Encyclopedia Americana.
Civilization to Coronium, page 89.
Clock.
An entry composed by F. A. B. Ward,
Science Museum, London.
Clock.
A machine that indicates or records the time of day
by dividing the earth's period of rotation
as accurately as possible
into equal time intervals.
Conventionally the period is divided into 24 hours,
each hour into 60 minutes,
and each minute into 60 seconds.
All clocks do this by means of some kind of
regular motion
that governs the indicating or recording elements
so that they make equal movements
in equal intervals of time.

*She skims down.*

DAL
Early Nonmechanical Clocks.
Egypt.
Sundials.
Water clocks.
Greece and Rome.
China.
Europe.
Sandglasses.

*She skims down and turns a page.*

DAL
Mechanical Clocks.
The first of all mechanical clocks known were
probably made about 1300.
They were large iron-framed structures,
driven by weights.
The cyclic motion they utilized was produced by
an escapement
known as the verge and foliot.

*She keeps skimming.*

DAL
The function of these first mechanical clocks
was not to indicate the time on the dial,

but to drive dials that gave astronomical indications,
and to sound the hour.

LUA
Please come out from under the table.

DAL closes the book.

LUA
Please come out from under the table.
I said come out.
Come out.
You need to eat something.

*DAL doesn't move.*

LUA
Fine, stay there.

She takes away the food and washes up.

LUA
(*speaking very rapidly*)
Dal does not know how to communicate.
She does not know how to listen.
This misfortune is not her fault;

something simply went wrong in her brain.
Listening, after all, is a privilege, an acquired skill
that can only be maintained by those of us
whose neurons and families are in certain categories
from the start.
My name is Lua.
The word "lua" is Portuguese.
The word "lua" means "moon."
I am lucky to be a very privileged person.
I am lucky to be a very, very good listener.
Dal is somewhat but not quite fully aware that
her brain is crowded, crowded, crowded.
Crowded with words.
The words in her mind dissolve and merge
with the words that she hears and reads,
the way fluids blend and bleed into each other.
This creates a mental flood:
a natural disaster
which continuously spills out of her mouth.
Continuously.
When she sleeps, she dreams in streaming text.
And when she's awake, I'm afraid to say,
she is simply a sea of nonsense.
The problem is, evolution stopped a long time ago.
Quite frankly, I am at a loss.
Quite frankly, she is deteriorating.

This property really ought to be sold.
She is far, far, far too dysfunctional to maintain it
alone.

*LUA drops a glass.*
*It breaks.*
*She shrieks.*

*Porous space.*

# SCENE 16

*Waning Crescent Moon.*

*DAL's eyes transfix on the broken glass.*
*She reaches out to touch a piece.*
*The sight of her suddenly startles LUA.*

LUA
Who are you?

DAL
Who are you?

LUA
I live here.
This is my house.
I don't know who you are.
You're trespassing in my house.

DAL
This is my house, too.
I live here with you.

LUA
This is my house.
You're trespassing in my house.
I don't know who you are.

*DAL carefully picks up and examines the broken glass.*

DAL
Look at how—
You're spelling—
You're making words // out of—

LUA
I'm the—
I nearly—
What am I talking about?
What can I say?
I live here.
I know this.

*LUA laughs.*

LUA
I live here with you.
I clean and narrate.

I clean up and narrate your life.
It's very important that I do this.
I'm extracting the jumble from your brain.
I'm creating space for cognition.

DAL
I have plenty of space.

*DAL lays the broken glass piece by piece on the table.*

LUA
I'm here to compartmentalize.
To categorize.
To help you think.
I'm here to sweep.
I'm here to vacuum.
I know this.

DAL
I don't need anything vacuumed.

LUA
I think,
I think that—

DAL
What?

LUA
What am I trying to say?

DAL
What are you trying to say?

LUA
I think that—
I think—

*DAL is distracted by her own hand.*
*It is bleeding.*

LUA
I think that—
I just think—
What I really want to tell you is—

*LUA's eyes fall to DAL's hand.*

LUA
I've cut myself.
I'm bleeding.

Would you like a bandage?
Let me get you a bandage.

*LUA exits.*

## SCENE 17

*DAL digs a hole and plants an encyclopedia*
*in the ground.*
*She proceeds to plant each encyclopedia*
*in the same way,*
*one by one, like flowers.*

*LUA reenters with fistfuls of medical supplies—*
*bandages, gauze, hydrogen peroxide, etc.*
*She forgets what she's doing.*
*She forgets where she is.*

LUA
What did I—?

*She sees DAL and drops everything on the table.*
*She begins resetting the kitchen to cook, but nothing is where*
*she's used to finding it.*

| LUA | DAL |
|---|---|
| 29 days, 12 hours, | 29 days, 12 hours, |
| and 44 minutes ago, | and 44 minutes ago, |
| somebody— | |
| | somebody passed— |
| somebody planted— | |

You told—
You told me—

    You told me—
    How to know—

She does not know
how to talk to people.

    If we can't speak—
    What I really want
    to tell you is—

She is a muddle
of symptoms.
She is lost in
her own world.
She clearly has spiraled
out of control
into some kind of
mental disorder.

    Your body is orbiting

    the earth right now,
    in fragments.

I am here
to take care of her.
I just—
I just think—
It's a mental flood.
A natural disaster.
What do you do
with their mail?
dots.
Bills.

    I promised to take care—
    I just—
    I just think—
    A map of our sleep.
    Glass boat.

    A million tiny colored

    Birds.

Crowded, crowded,
crowded.
How to reconcile—

Their birthday parties.
Their frames of reference.
Jumble.
I'm here to vacuum.
This misfortune—
Tragic—
Everything current—
Clocks.
Bills.
Categories.
This neglected field.
This neglected house.
Where did they go?

I don't know if I can—
What I really want
 to tell you is—
(LUA, c't)
29 days, 12 hours,
and 44 minutes—
I—
I just think—

They're making up
stories about you—
There, fresh flowers—
There, a letter—
Outer space—
Here, a vacuum.
Here, a covering.
Traveling through—
Space without matter—
Clicks.
Bells.
Categories.
A million epitaphs.
A field of pianos.
Solid, liquid, and gas
state properties.
Do you think you can—
What I really want
to tell you is—
(DAL, c't)
29 days, 12 hours,
and 44 minutes—
I just think—
I—

We are experimenting       We are toasting
with different medications.  empty glasses.
We do not know how to      We do not know how to—

articulate coherent thoughts.
When I open my mouth—

DAL
Absence pours out.

*LUA opens her mouth.*
*Thousands and thousands of wildflowers tumble out,*
*softly, swiftly.*

DAL
What I really want to tell you is—

LUA
What I really want to tell you is,
29 days, 12 hours, and 44 minutes ago—

DAL
Somebody—

LUA
Somebody told somebody—

DAL
Somebody planted—

LUA
Somebody said—

DAL
Somebody saw—

LUA
When I open my mouth—

DAL
Memory pours out.

*LUA opens her mouth and a flock of birds flies out of it.*
*They are countless, swift, and sweeping.*
*The entire world is engulfed with birds,*
*everywhere birds, for maybe 10 seconds.*
*Then all of the activity disperses as quickly as it appeared.*
*It begins to rain.*

DAL
For the past month—

LUA
It's been raining saltwater.

## SCENE 18

*LUA picks up an encyclopedia and reads.*

LUA
Encyclopedia Americana.
M to Mexico City, page 277.
Map.
An entry composed by D. B. Cole of the University
of Northern Colorado.
Map.
Any geographic image or physical representation
of the environment,
drawn to scale,
usually on a flat surface.
The term chart is most often applied to maps
of the sea,
or at least to maps used by sailors and fliers.
Map, a broader term, refers more particularly
to a representation of land.
The science of making maps is called cartography.
The word map comes from the Latin mappa
meaning "napkin" or "cloth,"
and the word chart comes from the Greek chartos,
which means "leaf" or "sheet of paper."

*She skims down.*

LUA
Remote Sensing.
Nonphotographic sensors
in the ultraviolet, infrared, visible, and microwave
spectra
and the modern development of electronic
processing and satellites
have all become important
in the gathering of data for mapmaking.
Scanning devices such as radar
detect energy from one small element of the
landscape at a time.
Because remotely-sensed images are recorded
in various tones of grays or colors,
identifying objects on imagery is usually more
difficult
than recognizing symbols on a map.

*She skims down.*

LUA
Imagery Sources.
Compilation.
Symbols.

Lettering.
"Lettering."
Lettering is one of the most significant features
of a map,
and particular emphasis must be given
to the styles, sizes, and positioning of the type.

*She looks up.*

LUA
This month is—
Today is—
What time is—?

# SCENE 19

*New Moon.*

LUA
I organize my senses into balloons.
I put my senses inside.
They are valentines.

My sense of sight goes first, in pink.

My sense of smell goes second, in orange.

My sense of taste goes third, in green.

My sense of hearing goes fourth, in yellow.

My sense of touch goes last, in blue.

I think about everything.
I'm emptied of everything.

*The rain increases to a downpour.*

SCENE 20

*The rain continues.*
*DAL sits at the table.*
*LUA looks for the moon.*

LUA
The moon is invisible.

DAL
What I really want to tell you is—

LUA
When she opens her mouth—


*The tick of a clock.*
*They wait.*


END

**Rachel Jendrzejewski** is a writer and interdisciplinary artist who works throughout the U.S. and internationally, most often investigating awareness, embodied experience, and the complexities of "community." She frequently collaborates with dancers, visual artists, musicians, fellow writers, and alleged non-artists to explore new performative vocabularies. Her work has been developed and/or presented by the Walker Art Center, Red Eye Theater, Public Functionary, Padua Playwrights, and Institute of Contemporary Art/Boston, among others. She is a Core Writer at The Playwrights' Center and holds an M.F.A. in Playwriting from Brown University. Learn more at rachelka.com and join her circle of supporters at patreon.com/rachelka.

**thank you**

To all of the artists and institutions who played such critical roles in shaping this play throughout its development process; to Erik Ehn, Lisa D'Amour, Theo Goodell, Lindsay Eller, Amy DeLap Jendrzejewski, Andrew Jendrzejewski, Ingrid Jendrzejewski, and The Playwrights' Center for extraordinary support in the writing process; to my Patreon circle for making so much possible; and to John Colburn and Spout Press for this beautiful book.